smoking lovely

smoking lovely

by Willie Perdomo

rattapallax press
new york city

Some of these poems have originally appeared in the following publications: *Urban Latino, Step Into A World: A Global Anthology of the New Black Literature, Bomb Magazine, Centro: A Journal for the Center for Puerto Rican Studies at Hunter College, Mosaic Literary Magazine, Listen Up: A Spoken Word Anthology, The United States of Poetry, Envoy* (Hunter College), *Long Shot, Rio Del Sol.com, Bum Rush the Page: A Def Poetry Jam Anthology, Role Call: A Generational Anthology of Social and Political Black Literature and Art, Untold Magazine, African Voices, Postcards of El Barrio* (Isla Negra Press), *Rattapallax Magazine,* and Russell Simmons' *ONE WORLD MAGAZINE*

Rattapallax Press
532 La Guardia Place, Suite 353
New York, NY 10012   USA
email: info@rattapallax.com / www.rattapallax.com
Ram Devineni, Publisher

Jacket Art: De La Vega. Jacket photo: Rene Flores. Author photo: Natasha Carrizosa. Music production by (David Rodriguez) dj mafioso for Needledrop Productions. Additional production work by Edwin Torres.

ISBN: 1-892494-61-2 (paperback)
ISBN: 1-892494-62-0 (e-book)

LIBRARY OF CONGRESS CATALOGING-IN-PUBLICATION DATA
Smoking Lovely / Willie Perdomo, author; ISBN: 1-892494-61-2 (pbk)
1. Poetry 2. Urban Poetry 3. World Poetry 4. Compact Disk
5. Hip-Hop 6. Spoken-Word 7. Urban Studies & Literature
I. Perdomo, Willie. II. Title.

First Edition: October 2003 / Second Edition: April 2005
LCCN: 2003092219

Willie Perdomo is the author of *Where a Nickel Costs a Dime*. His work has appeared in several anthologies including *The Harlem Reader, Poems of New York* and *Metropolis Found*. His work has also been published in *The New York Times Magazine, Bomb,* and *Pen America: A Journal for Writers and Readers*. He is the author of *Visiting Langston,* a Coretta Scott King Honor Book for Children, illustrated by Bryan Collier and has been featured on several PBS documentaries including *Words in Your Face* and *The United States of Poetry* as well as HBO'S *Def Poetry Jam* and BET's *Hughes's Dream Harlem*. He is currently working on his next book, *Emergency Money*.

Felix: Oscar, "the fault lies not in our stars but in ourselves."
Oscar: Shakespeare.

The Odd Couple

"I'ma tell you like this. Everybody here got at least three niggas fucked up on drugs in their family. And real shit is real shit."

DMX, *XXL Magazine Interview,* August 24, 2002

TABLE OF CONTENTS

CD LISTING

Artwork on CD and cover by De La Vega

Lexington Avenue Prelude

Your breath is getting further away from
one more chance
The other side is getting closer
A voice over there is telling you that it's
not now but right now
You have become the real dream keeper
Falling deeper and deeper
into the friendly skies
This is the face-to-face appointment with
the Department of Human Resources that you
can't miss even if you tried
The last bag you sniffed
was cut with hyperspace because
your face just popped out of a
black sky and it looked like
King Tut with a shape up
The bomb has dropped and the
Fania All-Stars are coming through
the static in the kitchen radio
Ahora vengo yo
Sing about the graffiti tags that have
been washed away by acid rain
Riff on the bodegas that have been
blown up by missiles
Twist it one time for the community
centers that have been demolished by
empowerment zones
Your boys always said that the day
would come when you went out like
La Lupe and Charlie Parker put together
Bankrupt with your heartbreak and thuggery

in a box set of CDs and everybody on the
block is talking about you with a "but" after
everything like he coulda been but that
nigga was bad but yeah ese cabron cantaba but
the mic is on and it's time
You need to get up there and
give it away so you can keep it

Dedication

for my wife Sandra
who gives me love
like the song —
all the way

for BJ —
the hope

for my son Neruda —
a love supreme

and for my anonymous
brothers and sisters
who are still looking for
just one more

Smoking Lovely

When you smoke crack
Everything is measured by

How fast your face melts.
If I can pull your eyes

Out of their sockets and
Your cheekbones bruise me

When I hug you or your
Lips scratch mine when we

Kiss then you must be
Smoking lovely.

Spotlight at the Nuyorican Poets Café

Finally fixed
I get to the café
in time for my spotlight.
I ask Julio the Bouncer if
he's gonna stay inside to
hear me read tonight.
He says only if I read something happy,
none of that dark ghetto shit because
tonight's crowd got him pissed. He is
the best random judge in the house as he
soothes a low scoring slam poet.
"C'mon, you know you can't
take this shit too seriously."
Julio strengthens my aesthetic as I
walk through the door and spot the
spoken word racketeers who
get close enough to dig into my
pockets when I fall asleep.
I just spent my last ten dollars
and they look at me stupid when
I ask if they can spare some
real change.

I was just a poet
wanting to read a poem
the first night I came here.
Since then
I have become a street poet
then somebody's favorite urban poet
a new jack hip-hop rap poet
a spoken word artist
a born-again Langston Hughes
a downtown performance poet
but you won't catch me rehearsing,
my spit is ready made real.

I walk up to the cherubic man with white hair
whose smile will not close until the
poetry café is torn down;
who will allow himself to die
only when love fails to create.
He starts telling me stories about
his soul brother
Miky the Junkie Christ
Creator of the ghetto Genesis where
Shit begat fucked up.
Saint Miguelito who saw God and said,
"Vayaaa! Papa Dio! Wassup?
I heard you got the good shit."
The cherubic man with white hair stays
alive by sniffing Miky's ashes
in the Avenue B air.

I go to the back of the bar
and sit next to the blind man who's
waiting for me to light his cigarette.
"Where you been you jive nigga you?
I'm glad you here
cuz these muthafuckas wanna cop pleas
and sell Cliff notes before they
read a goddamn thing."
A guest poet from the academy
is invited to the stage.
He begs the audience to be gentle because
his work is really built for the page.
The blind man tells him to
shut up
and read the goddamn poem.

I kiss the lady with the sunglasses,
sometimes used to deflect rays,
always to look where I can't see.
She's been taking notes on the scene,
watching poets exchange business cards
as they tap dance toward the stage.
She takes a moment to hug me tight and
begs me to take care of myself because the
bigger picture needs me.

The impresario leaps onto the stage,
grabs the mic and tells the DJ to give him a
hippiddy hop and a hippiddy ho,
"Is Word Perfect in the house?!"
The flame on a white prayer candle above
the bar is doing the Cucaracha.
In the photo portrait behind it,
Miky is looking dead into the camera.
Before I reach the mic
the good Reverend Pedro hands me
a condom and says, "Here, man.
You never know what you might
catch up there."

The Day Hector Lavoe Died

The baritone Univision broadcast came from the living room TV.

"En las noticias hoy, El Cantante de Los Cantantes, Hector Lavoe, murió en — "

Mami Cuca yells from her dent in the sofa, where the world is a *telenovela*, where she can book flights to Miami and Mexico and get lost in other people's drama. "Papo! Mira! Hector Lavoe!"

She knows that I will stop to see the voice that helped me sing my own song about *mi gente en El Barrio y la vida de las putas, los tecatos y las brujas, los dichosos, los tiburones, los cantantes y los soneros, los bodegueros, las gatas, los perros y las matas en las ventanas de los projectos* in English.

I rub the funk out of my eyes and suck in all the dope that's nesting at the top of my nasal passage. I walk into the living room and Mami Cuca points to the TV.

"Miralo, mijo. Se murió. He died. Look at him. He was the best of the best, and look how he wasted away." She starts telling that story about the morning Hector Lavoe came to pick up my Uncle Lolé who could rip the skins off a bongo. She had to throw them out for trying to start a mainline bang-bang in the bathroom.

I sink into the love seat near the sofa and join the *coro* during Technicolor footage of a young Fania All-Star. He is smiling at us through hazel tinted eyeglasses. He is dressed in a pearl-white three piece suit, silk shirt and a giant red bow tie. We stand in a stadium, singing and clapping along to his *comedia* tragic. The broadcast cuts to a hospitalized *salsero*, lying twisted under sterile white bed sheets, sunglasses too big for his face, waving to us with the strength he had to spare.

"Coño, que flaco," I say.

"Como tú , *mantecoso*," Mami Cuca says. "Just like you. You know why he's like that, right? You know, right?" She gives me the answer by miming an injection into the crook of her elbow.

After the retrospective I go back to my room and sniff my breakfast bag; the bag that gets my tank off "E." I turn off the lights, sit on my fold-up chair and Hector sings to me in a closing tribute. *Que problema, caballeró / en que me encuentro yo.* Mami Cuca continues her commentary on the breaking news. "Just like you. He didn't have a monkey on his back. He had King Kong, baby."

My nod comes and takes me to a parade. I hear a blast of trumpets, a wave of trombones, and I change my direction. I follow the sun as it funnels its way through a cool black sky. *Viejos* stop slapping their dominoes, radios are turned off, *bochinche* vines stop flowing, *bodega* gates come slamming down and I finally get to see my uncle play. He is sitting on a park bench with a conga between his legs. A woman next to me does not realize her hips are moving until she lets out a loud moan, asking for more. My uncle tells me that this is where he's been spending the rest of his life. I ask him if we can collaborate as I do backstrokes in the drip coming down my throat. I hear a long cigarette ash fall and tap the linoleum. Mami Cuca is talking to herself about salsa and love. Her slippers drag to the bathroom. The water pills are working extra hard today. She hums a bolero riff and bangs on my door without calling for me, making sure I'm not drowning in my vomit. I clear my throat and sigh cuz she fucked up my high with that same story about all that could've been in a world where the only thing left to sing about is a woman putting on her nightgown, talking about that Mother's Day when Hector Lavoe sang "El Todopoderoso" at the annual St. Paul's dance. She said that even the saints came down from their stained glass windows and started dancing.

Tenderloin

The guy in the tweed blazer says he came west to chill.

Johnny Shakespeare from New York City.

He works his jones like a natural birth control cycle: every two days he comes to shoot tar and watch snow on Ron's second-hand TV.

I wave him in from my cage where I sell rough toilet paper and give out old towels.

One day Johnny Shakespeare was late for his flight back home.

They can wait, he said.

He checked for his wallet as he watched an Aztec chief spray paint a self-portrait on a brick wall.

He had faith that love could still work when he got back East.

On the BART back to Oakland he went through his file of excuses.

The police put him in jail for talking to the ghost of Huey Newton on the top step of the Alameda County Courthouse.

He was trying to restore the face of the Virgin de Guadalupe.

He was kidnapped by a department store security squad who thought that he was a member of Al Qaeda.

He was mugged and had to read poems for train fare.

He met two girls who had a tweed blazer fetish.

He went to Fisherman's Wharf and recreated a romantic weekend he once had.

He needed to get his thoughts together so he walked up and down The Crookedest Street in the World.

He had a meeting with the local community board to let them know that Lake Merritt was filled with blood.

He turned into a penthouse panther and went prowling through the streets looking for someone to finance the revolution.

seesaw

spent a whole day and night
playing on my seesaw
see if I could forget
saw that it was over
before it started

I never change
the way I get over it
some brothers I know
buy a new CD or
join a new gym
sisters chop off their locks
order new magazines or
start practicing yoga

I go up in smoke
and come down in a nod
I go up in smoke
and come down in a nod

then I play
with my old journals
so I can hear myself
screaming for help
promising to stop
as soon as I finish
the last one
but beware
my foolish heart
wants to play forget again

so I go up in smoke
and come down in a nod
I go up in smoke
and come down in a nod
and I tell myself
that everything is alright
I can live without her
as long as I got
my seesaw

The Flood

When God sent
the flood
his mother said:

*"Mop that mess off
the floor, boy!"*

And God said:

*"That ain't mess, mami.
Those are tears. Some
for sorrow. Some for joy."*

You Pay For What You Get, But You Never Get What You Pay For

Brooklyn bound and I left my heart uptown with a Mexican mango sculptor. I should have known something was wrong when Satan stopped singing the blues in front of the Studio Museum of Harlem. Last night the queen of Sugar Hill slipped into a new storefront and ran off with the councilman who was up all night keeping his eyes on the prize.

The corners were taken over by corn row hustlers and kente cloth syndicates. Coffee chains, T-shirt clubs and ringing taco bells got the magazines saying that our communities are safe and clean, but the other day I kissed a girl who had a monster in her blood and didn't even know it.

Wrecking balls are aimed at the heads of housing projects. The world is getting baggy with brand names and producers are taking hip-hop speak seminars so they can help us keep it real. There's an invisible billboard on the side of the State Office building. It's a promotion for the platinum-selling single, "You Don't Have to Go Home (But You Got to Get the Fuck Out of Here)."

This morning buses disguised as historic neighborhood tours came and stole all the queen's brownstones. A homeless man went checking for leftovers. He walked by a silver-studded prophet who was preaching in front of a subway station and pointing to a star that had six points and he said, "Sheeet. Even if God did have an afro, I still ain't got nowhere to live."

Papo's Ars Poetica

I'm stuck in a poem that sounds like
the round of bullets you expect after
that sudden car screech on the avenue

This poem looks like a
mother who just lost her only son
to the last gunshot of the night
Her long cries sneak under my door
like the beginning of dinner

My eyes are buried inside this poem's
avenue like peeping tom traffic
lights checking out last night's
rite of passage painting a dog
chasing a cat with a jungle
boogie beat down for his ass

My teeth bite on this poem
like the slow wind that chews on
tomorrow's myths that brothers
are busy making on noontime
corners where my ears are
stashed on the down low
I heard Papo fell off like a
bad bag of dope

I'm stuck in this poem like a
squealing rat caught in a discount
glue trap soaking in a fresh puddle
of piss psst psst pssssssst mira mami

                              I'm home

in the street of this poem
where I'm stuck

New Jack City

Ain't nothing new about
New jack hustlers

They might be using
Computers to count

But they still hire
Guns for insurance

Franklin Avenue Snack Box

London fog covers
Eastern Parkway
Benches are drenched with
Colonial dew

I stop at the 99 cents store for some
Mistolin and soca
  get someteen
  and wave everybody...
And everything costs more than
A dollar
  get someteen and wave

I buy a ganja sack before
Beat cops turn the corner

West Indian Biggie's oxtails
Keep mami's pork chops
On the back burner

Bob Marley is a must
At the stolen CD sale

Big Black talking in penal jazz
Took a flat five
Last time he was in jail

The only Puerto Rican
Flag on the block
Looks like it's crying

British empire boots stomp on
No. 2 train shoulders

Angry nurses
Curse sick passenger delays
And whoever gave birth
To bomba clot boy

Hasidim stride by
African butter soap

Crusty crack heads
Get chased by pit bulls
For one more hit

Hairdressers take tonic
Juice breaks

I cradle my single man dinner
A thigh, a leg, and a bun
Waiting for the green light
A schoolgirl reads a gangster
Who calls her
His sun

Electronic Kites

I can't see your voice but I
Can hear your style when your
Electronic kites land in my box
It takes a while for me to reply
I've been writing poetry in the
Middle of marketing meetings
Looking for my own way to
Position our story
You tried to take it with you
Even when the classics said
That you couldn't
Your handmade journals were
Packed by size in your knapsack
And there still wasn't enough
Room in baggage claims for
What you left behind
There was a kiss that made
You feel like you were set up
The bridges that were laced
With moonlight pearls
It was poetry in a night where poets
Needed gimmicks to be heard and
All you needed was enough
Space to send the kind of love that's
Practiced by a political prisoner who
Refuses his get-out-of-jail-free card
Or to dream of holding me tight inside
The eye of a hurricane with a
Lyrical name and wake up to find
That all of it was real

French Roast

Jet lagged love making
Like dope dick sex
Hotel Tres Nicole
Is blessed now

French telephone ring ring
We finger draw on windows
Fogged with carnality

Central heating for
Rain breakfast

La Pigalle positions
Put some jelly
On her fresh croissant
Oooo la la tongue it
Right there

My funky mademoiselle
on the Boulevard San Michel
Striking expatriate poses
By the Seine

Nasty French *cabrona*
Works in American-style café
Says she don't know English
In English

Should Old Shit Be Forgot

Papo the Poet started kicking a
Poem while Dick Clark put the
City on the count

Once again we pledge down for
Whatever until the day we die
Love forever in one minute it takes
Sixty seconds to forget the one who
Left you waiting at the bus stop

And I was like:
All that shit you sayin'
Sounds good but let's
Talk about the thirty
Dollars you owe me

I hear you I hear you I hear
What you sayin'
We boys and we should
Be happy when big ass
Disco balls drop on
151 proof resolutions

Father Time says
He's only gonna smoke
On the weekends

New Year cornets
Are swept off the street
Like old friends

Champagne corks ricochet
Off ballroom walls

Roast pork burns while we
Puff and pass in project halls

Bullets kill El Barrio sky to
Celebrate holding it down
The same ole same ole shit we
Say every year
Fuck it
Pass that rum
It's cold out here
Who wants some?
You could say pleeze
You could freeze
Whatever
Happy New Years
Feliz Año Nuevo
I'm out here for a reason
Not the season
Should old shit be forgot
And all that good stuff
But I want my money
Before next year

Notes for a Slow Jam

The Notes

I wanted to play this like Petrarch and bless you with a suite of sonnets. But I can't rock sonnets, so I thought I would write you 100 letters for 100 days, but I'm getting discharged tomorrow morning so I'll say what I need to say on the back of this Patient Bill of Rights.

Yesterday my roommate asked me if I had a girlfriend out in the world. I told him about the night I watched you network a velvet lounge as Wynton Marsalis played a blues tribute for Albert Murray. During the solo I heard myself blow a quick *oh shit, who is that* riff, but that little voice that didn't like me convinced me that a woman whose laugh could play with music was too good for me.

My roommate said, "Damn, that's messed up," and went to the dayroom before I could tell him that the first time you and I made love we stood in bed for three days, had breakfast delivered, and listened to Robin Harris snap on Bebe's kids. I had your laugh all to myself.

Right now I'm looking out the window feeling the poem you always wanted about to drop like the heavy rain slapping the aluminum swing seats in Mount Morris Park. I see clearly through the tree-shaking thunder tapping the bell tower. Diamonds are dropping from the sky and I'm gonna play a solo before they call a melancholy snack time. Stray dogs bark at my soundproof window and I just hit my big bottom because the bass line dropped and all I want to know is: Where's my funny valentine?

The Slow Jam

This is the poem you always wanted
I've turned into a fire-can crooner
to sing you this slow jam
a farewell greeting
no sooner than the sun set
on our meeting I had a
song for you
but first I had to sample
from the midnight quiet storm
Break up to make up and
make up to break up and
break up to wake up
I was a three-time loser
persistent fell in heart over
head not even a chance to
carve the initials of our romance
on the bark of a tree
There was nothing no one left to
point at and say it's all because of you
so I had an encounter session with my
bathroom mirror and those black
crescents that real make-up under my eyes
couldn't cover the cries that fell on the
street as I peaked on a broken
heart binge had to get high so I buy a
bag and go to Angel's Social Club where I
found the answer boiling in a juke box
pick a song
hip-hoppin' through life
I thought salsa was just for
the rice and beans

I was wrong
You'd probably think
I was high right now
if I told you that Tito Rojas
was a Greek playwright and
that Euripides had his own band
Listen to the tragic hero
chillin' on the corner
epics and shit spillin' from his mouth
and the chorus the chorus is throwing
echoes off the rooftop
Here it comes:
The *corazón* break
ay ay ay
Y dicen que los hombres
nunca nunca nunca nunca
deben llorar/ay ay ay
and they say that the men
should never never never cry
I looked into the mirror
one more time
before I chased you away
and just in case you don't speak Spanish
I leave you sinking in some
Muddy Waters like you can't spend
what you ain't got and you can't lose
what you ain't never had
My pockets are empty
and I'm letting you go
without a fight
but before you go
here's the poem
you always wanted

Brother Lo and The Maxims

Police siren light splashed
Across Brother Lo's face
He got into his science-dropping stance
He lit a cigarette at a 45 degree angle
He puffed hard and exhaled a
Jet stream of smoke into the wind
And then he said:
Man in East Harlem lives
According to a set of maxims
What comes around goes around
That's a maxim
Like apples falling on your head
But more like you chilling on your stoop
Sipping on the dregs of a Mr. Softee vanilla shake
You tell your mother that you'll be right back
You turn to go and a face you thought you
Forgot is waiting for you with a Rambo knife
He sticks it into your solar plexus for that
Shit you did when you was a kid
What went around
Came around

Payback is a bitch
But revenge
Is a muthafucka
Like the first maxim
Except the mysterious mug wipes
The blade clean with your hair
He spits on you and
The last thing you hear is
Him laughing like the evil
Villain in a horror flick

Bullets ain't got no names
Lately you been trying to live on the down low
Getting off a train stop before yours
Saying no to party invitations and
Walking around the block
Instead of down the avenue
One night you decide to go to sleep early
You just finished writing a long love
Letter to your ex-girlfriend but your mother's
Boyfriend smoked your bedtime Newport
You go to Khadafi's 24-hour counter
You see Charlie Rock
He's running the block now
He asks you where you been because
Nobody been seeing you around
Just chillin' you say when the clapping starts
Shells tingle street stars slam your
Chest into a pool of hot sewing needles
Red stream sangre and rainbow oil puddles
Slow down the ice cream stick boat races
Somebody yells for your mother who just
Heard you whisper goodbye from the ceiling
You told your ex-girlfriend that you wanted death to
Be sure when it came to play but you got caught
By a bullet with no name

Oh Shit

I got a feeling my woman is playing me dirty
Said I got a feeling my woman is playing me dirty
Her declarations of love been awfully wordy

Forty-One Bullets Off-Broadway

It's not like you were looking at a
vase filled with plastic white roses
while pissing in your mother's bathroom
and hoped that today was not the day
you bumped into four cops who
happened to wake up with a bad
case of contagious shooting

From the Bronx to El Barrio
we heard you fall face first into
the lobby of your equal opportunity
forty-one bullets like silver push pins
holding up a connect-the-dots picture of Africa
forty-one bullets not giving you enough time
to hit the floor with dignity and
justice for all forty-one bullet shells
trickling onto a bubble gum-stained mosaic
where your body is mapped out

Before your mother kissed you goodbye
she forgot to tell you that American kids
get massacred in gym class
and shot during Sunday sermon
They are mourned for a whole year while
people like you go away quietly

Before you could show your
I.D. and say, "Officer — "
Four regulation Glock clips went achoo
and smoked you into spirit and by the
time a special street unit decided what was
enough another dream submitted an
application for deferral

It was la vida te da sorpresas/sorpresas
te da la vida/ay dios and you probably thought
I was singing from living la vida loca
but be you prince/be you pauper
the skin on your drum makes you
the usual suspect around here

By the time you hit the floor
protest poets came to your rescue
legal eagles got on their cell phones
and booked red eyes to New York
File folders were filled with dream team
pitches for your mother who was on TV
looking suspicious at your defense
knowing that Justice has been known
to keep one eye open for the right price

By the time you hit the floor
the special unit forgot everything they
learned at the academy
The mayor told them to take a few
days off and when they came back he
sent them to go beat up a million young
black men while your blood seeped through
the tile in the lobby of your equal
opportunity from the Bronx to El Barrio
there were enough shots to go around

Ten Pound Draw

On my first trip to London
I learned that the best way to
see the city is from the top
of a red double-decker bus
If you want to be loved on the
first night in more than one
position you have to help with
the cooking

On my second trip to London
I learned that the best way to
get your smoke on was to first
find out where the dark faces live
I rode the Tube to Brixton Station
and found them all over the world
living at the end of the line

At the top of the escalator
a brother selling oils and incense
sends orders into his cell phone
You think righteousness must be
a booming market

The black girls the blahk girls
The black girls on the block
smile and insist that I am Pakistani
when I tell them that I'm Nuyorikistani
so I talk como like this y como like
that y como like kikireeboo tan linda
no doubt it's all good
I am all of that if you want me to be
but do you know where I can find
a ten-pound draw

No luck finding the parliament funk
and Roger in Reading said I can't
ask for a dime bag so I buy ten
bottles of Egyptian musk and show
Brotherman the thirst in my eyes
He leads me to the smoke
for a small finders fee

I am willing to take these chances
in spite of the suspicious glances
but just in case I buy a Big Ben postcard
address it to The Crazy Bunch
c/o El Barrio and write:
"Yo, if I don't make it back home
I was thinking about y'all
when I went to this place called Brixton
looking for a ten-pound draw"

black boots

title for a jazz
riff a catwalk
strut Fifth Avenue
stroll black
boot leather
bass fashion
mama look
good as

hell

Stop Signs

I started this poem
on the ride back to Heathrow
It could have been the A train to the Bronx
but the stars in the magazine
would have said the same thing
Cancer has difficult choices ahead
Aries finds romance in unlikely places

I felt like telling you that I'm not sure
how one is supposed to read the signs
unless they're falling all over you
If it was up to me I would grab
the ones that shoot across the sky
shake them hard one time
blow on them for good luck
and let them roll
But I had to catch myself before I
slipped and broke something so
I flipped it one time
If you can be with the one you love
Don't love the one you're with

In the middle of Piccadilly Circus
Eros was pointing the wrong way
Cool ass swans broke off into
schools of six and suggested that I
leave you a note before my flight
Damn your Spanish was good, too
Hablas Español?
Sí.
Te quiero.
Y yo te quie-roh too.

I laughed through the turbulence replaying
That day I called you "mami" by mistake
even after you told me that you ain't into
that papi thing
you know that ay papi sí papi cojelo
papi que es tuyo papi thing
and I told you yes mami
it's okay, sugar
I can call you honey, baby
Don't you know you my
sweetheart, boo?

Shit to Write About

The last time Kriptonite stopped me on Lexington Avenue was the night he had a bottle fight with his girlfriend. He asked me to write something sweet for her. He said it should be something like the poem I wrote for Spy's girl on Valentine's Day. He asked me to recite the poem. The poem went like this:

The longer I look
for something to say
the harder I search
for another way to
show you my love
I don't have a rose
or a box of chocolates
to send in place of
my heart
but I can start
with a bouquet of
I love you and I miss you
close your eyes and
feel me kiss you
If I could I would turn into
a greeting card
and send myself express
but all I have is this poem
to show that I love you
more than I love you less

Krip yelled, "Yeah, yeah, that's the shit I'm talking about! But I want mine to be better than that, you know what I'm sayin'?"

"Tell me what you miss about your girl, Krip," I said.

"You know how she puts me to sleep? She sings me lullabies while she writes her name in cursive on my bare back with the tips of her fingernails. She loves it when I tell her to sit in front of me so I can run a comb real soft through her hair. I miss my girl, yo," he said like he was lost for the first time.

It reminded me of the night we were standing in front of 1990 and Krip pointed to a cardboard shrine on the corner. And then he pointed to a row of Air Jordans hanging off the neck of a light post; the glow-in-the-dark rosaries hanging off red candles with eternal flames; untapped for-ties and unwrapped cigars: 'hood libations for our mans and them, who may they rest in peace as we leave "R.I.P." burning on the wall and visit their tombstones daily. And Krip said, "Now if you gonna write about something, that's some shit to write about."

Today he stopped me because his subject was life stories; unauthorized biographies about players who are reaching the end of their game.

"Yo, I been looking all over Lexington for you, man. I heard you was living in Brooklyn now. Coño, you getting fat, kid. Que Dios te bendiga, mano. Word up. Last time I saw you, you looked like you was smoking lovely. Not for nothin' but everybody thought you was down with the dead poet's society. Kenny Mac told me that you was getting paid to write your life story and like I been having these scrambling nights and hand-to-mouth baby crying mornings. I just lost my mother to the Monster and I'm waiting for a formula that I can drink to grow stronger. Our boys are getting blown off the corners like ghost town dirt. I keep running when the cages get closer, crying when no one is looking, feel-ing like every day is gonna be the last time I see my son and then I start-ed thinking, if I wanted to write a book how much you think my life would be worth?"

December

She said, *You found the small key.*

He was hidden in her dusty high school diaries.

The sex was so good that he had to pump new breath into his lungs.

They shared a cigarette after she offered him a view from her pink duvet.

Risking rickets they waited for a cab on the top step of her brownstone.

The cold cracked her chapped lips.

They kept kissing and kissing.

Wind-chill factors turned her eyes into a bolero.

Open Mic at Make the Road By Walking, Inc.

— Caminante, no hay camino. Se hace el camino al andar.
(Searcher, there is no road. We make the road by walking.) —
Antonio Machado

If it all starts at home
Then you're grateful
When your students present you
With a cherry blossom bouquet
Stolen from a manicured
Bronxville station garden

Back in Bushwick
Running freely through blocks
Stained with family recipes
They finally discover metaphor
J.R. says that he is so glad to
Be out of that white boy air

The open mic starts with a
Ballet on a cinder block stage
The first rap song said that there was
Broken glass everywhere
These road makers feed each
Other big bowls of locks and pops
If you're not careful
You can have your heart
Snatched from its socket
Sprinkled on a tobacco leaf
Rolled up and smoked

The day care picture book readers
Ring rosies and duck gooses
Around plastic pink chairs

You know you are in the right place
Where struggle is bilingual and
Over-worked workers of the world
Can only afford guitar licks to
Pay their membership dues

You hope that the jokes on
Dirty sneakers and generic blue jeans
Will not lead to a vicious paper chase
That when the roads are finally made
The corner drugstore cowboys will be
Left without their cocktail rocks and
Quicksilver last words so that when
Foreign documentary makers visit
Us with lab reports that erase the
High octave lean of our baseball caps
The hip-hop of our new sun language
We will look into the camera and
Recite the next line of poetry by which
The world will choose to live

Word to Everything I Love

I feel like dropping some bombs tonight
I have a milk crate bursting at the handles with
Muses that look like 3 x 7 memo pads but
I only need a minute of your time
If I told you that your woman was playing you dirty
And you asked me if I was for real
I would say, Word
Word to everything I love
Because that's what Brother Lo and them say
When they want you to believe them
More than you believe in the god of your choice
These poets who don't even know it
Will not put their palms
On a stack of black bibles
Or swear on the soul of an unborn child
If you find out they're lying
You can have everything they love

Here's bomb number one:
I want to give a shout out
To all those lyric poets
Who got low scores and left the short circuit
Through the back door
This is my word to everything I love
When you come back home
You expect welcome mats of damn
Where you been?
You look good
Is there anything I can do for you?
Anything you need?
But these are the same mats
You stepped on before
When you come back home

You expect the spotlight to be as bright
As the last time you got on stage
But the page flipped
And you got left out the next chapter
When you come back home
Everybody asks you if
You're working your steps
You say you closed your eyes
Took one giant step
And never looked back
Word to everything I love
This is what I'm telling you
After you make the love you dream of making
You come home to clean your closets
And make sure to keep the phone nearby
Just in case you bump into half of something
That will bring you back and
Hit you where it hurts

This blockbuster I give to the word hitters
Shadowboxing backstage
Making sure the last line fits
Let me a make a short story long
I want to tell you about the night I walked her
To an all-night Pathmark
It was snowing so much that
I felt like I was in a souvenir globe
The whole Goya bean section knew that we were in love
I carried her garlic, ginger and twist-off mop in one hand
Orange juice and scented candles in the other
She gave me her tongue in the vestibule and
Told me a secret
The next night we met in a garden filled with computers

We downloaded all kinds of flowers and trees
Word, word to everything I love
A few weeks later
Someone had sent her mouth
A giant AOL Instant Message smile
She roller-bladed to the clinic with Chuito de Bayamon
Blasting on her headphones
Don't you understand?
This is for you repeat offenders
In the final round
Who need new material
The song of the almost was
The call you get on the life line
Sounds like tears dropping into a voicemail
She would have wanted to wear ponytails to class picture day
She would have sketched a poem and left it on my pillow
She was surrounded by a circle of street pigeons in a city square
I miss train stops thinking of what her name
Would have been

The New Boogaloo

there's a disco ball
spinning starlight on
the New Boogaloo

tell Sonia
that the bombs
are ready to drop
that we got *soneros*
ready to sing
to those flowers
that did not survive
Operation Green Thumb

tell Dwight
that the renaissance
he's been looking for
is ready to set up shop
that dreams are starting
to take responsibility
for themselves

tell Marcito
that painters are eating *piraguas*
sitting on milkcrates
and kickin' it with poets
who are bored
with keeping it real

tell Rosalia
that the Reverend Pedro
is on the rooftop
handing out passports
because the spaceship *casita*
is about to take off

oye mamita
no te apures
que como like a
Brook Avenue *bombaso*
we gonna make you dance
que como un cocotaso limpio
we gonna make your head rock

so tell Pachanga
that si no hablas español
bienvenido
that si no hablas inglés
beinvenido

and don't forget to
tell Domingo
that we're gonna shoot it up
mainline
mainland
mainstream
underground
until we catch your vein
so take this sound
to the grave
and tell the whole block
that a *bámbula*
building session
is about to begin
and it's gonna be like
two church boys
talking loud on the train
praising the Lord
in espanglish hip-hop speak
check it:

pero que son
yo se que fui the Lord son
eso que mira you know
what it is fam
we keep the Bible real, kid
tu me entiende
pero que he wants me to learn
because he told me sun
to bring my notebook sun
to all the sermons sun
y mira I was like whoa
when the reverend Pedro
was waiting for me
with a passport
and he told me
that this time
we gonna die knowing
how beautiful
we really are

Poet Looking For Free Get High

I just came off a mountain where I used to get high by looking at a hawk spread his wings and take over the sky with a gangster lean. I lost my breath one morning when I saw the snow-covered trees turn silver a second before the day broke into something new. But I keep coming back to this poem like roses are red and violets are blue for the lady who came rushing out of my building, digging sleep out of the corner of her eyes. There used to be a day when her smile could make rain go away and her voice could heal you into building a new heart.

"What's up girl, you still out here?" I asked as she walked by.

"I'm just waiting for the nightmare to end, baby," she said, stopping by a side-view mirror to apply a new coat of cherry-flavored lip gloss. Humming something like you've forgotten the words I love you she walked onto the avenue and announced a grand opening.

Lately, my girl has been crying because she's happy. She used to work under the red lights. I hand her a fresh loaf of Italian bread for the ham and eggs and tell her that it's time for me to stop writing about Snow White, Big Leslie, Honey, Cinderella and them. I pour myself a glass of ginger ale and watch the kids in the playground turn gold through the sparkling soda. A bronze seal provides a steady sprinkle of water on their scream songs.

After breakfast we fell asleep listening to *Salsa con Polito.* I dreamt that we woke up to breaking news. DJ Polito Vega interrupted the broadcast to announce that I found a new voice. My girl said I can't throw it back in God's face. I can't steal it like I stole sleep from my mother. Now you can get high and it won't cost you anything, pa, she said. She kissed me on my forehead and asked me to help her break in the new love seat.

It's been a long time since I paid for that dream where I never hit the floor. I can feel the old poems dying in the ole' if it ain't rough it ain't right sanitation trucks pissing on the street 'round midnight. It cost me more than I could afford to get to the bottom of things without paying a fare.

Crazy Bunch Barbecue at Jefferson Park

This is definitely for
the brothers who ain't here
who woulda said
I had to write a poem
about this get together
like a list of names on a
memorial that celebrated
our own Old-Timer's Day

For those of us
who age in hood years
where one night can equal
the rest of your life and
surviving the trade-off was
worth writing on the wall
and telling the world
that we were here
forever

The barbecue started with a
snap session
Jerry had the best snap of the day
when he said that my family
was so poor and the fellas said
how poor and he said so poor that
on Thanksgiving they had to buy
turkey-flavored Now & Laters
The laughter needed no help when
we exposed the stretch marks of
our growing pains

Phil had barbecue on the grill
He slapped my hand when I tried to
brush extra sauce on a chicken leg

Yo, go find something to do
write a poem
write something
do something
I got this
I'm the chef
you the poet
talk about how you glad to be here
look at that little boy on the baseball diamond
look at him run circles around second base
today is his birthday
write about how the wind is
trying to take his red balloon

It use to take a few shots of
something strong before we
could cry and say I love you
we have always known how
to curse and bless the dead
now we let the silence say it
and like the little boy's sneakers
disappearing in a cloud of dirt
we walk home in the sun
grown up and full

This is definitely for
the brothers who ain't here
who woulda said
I had to write a poem
about this get together
like a list of names on a
memorial that celebrated
our own Old-Timer's Day

For those of us
who age in hood years
where one night can equal
the rest of your life and
surviving the trade-off was
worth writing on the wall
and telling the world
that we were here
forever

Writing About What You Know

I.

A young Puerto Rican boy named Papo is on a class trip to the Aguilar Branch of the New York Public Library on 110th Street in East Harlem. His name is Papo because 7 out of every 10 brothers in El Barrio, Los Sures in Williamsburg, Loisaida, Brook Avenue, Humboldt Park in Chicago and most of Willimantic, Connecticut are named Pito, Papo, Flaco, Chino, Piloto, Chano, or Waneko. These are names that will make you dream of Taino warriors in battle with Spaniard conquistadors.

Up and down the block there are jingles for *manteca, yuca, tamarindo, metadona, plátano maduro y pan caliente* and Papo is listening to the Head Librarian lecture on the value of learning the Dewey Decimal System. "If you need something on Earth Science, you first go to the card catalog and" — but all Papo can hear is the wahwahwahwahwah of urgent police sirens speeding toward the projects.

He turns his head toward the one-week Express Book section. There's a book with a picture of his block on the cover. He can tell by the identification tags on the wall telling him who loved who and for how long. The book says that there is poetry inside. The title buzzes on Papo's tongue like a biscuit of neon announcing instant Lotto and liquor. The poet is standing in the reflection of a lamp post that beams on Puerto Rican flags dangling chest forward out of tenement windows. Cuchifrito stands blink their 24-hour florescent crowns for the late night tree blazers who end their cipher sessions with a taste for un relleno de papa and a large cup of sesame seed juice.

"Excuse me, Luis. It's not polite to walk away while the librarian is talking," says Ms. Diaz.

Papo says, "I just wanted to see that book over— "

"You can see it when she's finished," says Ms. Diaz.

The next day Papo brings his father to the library because only adults can check the book out.

II.

Papo tells his Creative Writing teacher that he's having a difficult time finding something to write about. The teacher says, *Write about what you know. And remember: don't tell me, show me.*

That night he was chillin' in front of Caridad's Grocery with Baby Face Nelson and Green-Eye Raymond. A silver BMW drives by with a jukebox in the trunk. The Yellow-Top Crew just cracked their first bottle of champagne. The tempo for Papo's first assignment will be set by a round of Uzi shots ringing off the Wagner Project rooftops. The shots are supported by a heavy, deep, hip-hop jeep, bass line thump with a stream of furious congas keeping rhythm in the background, warning you to strap in and hold on tight.

Green-Eye Raymond: Sounds like they pullin' somebody's wig back in Wagner, sun. How many shots you heard?

Papo: Like ten.

Baby Face Nelson: Word. That's what I heard. And those shots sounded like they had names and addresses.

After the ambulance and police come to break the set, the streets go back to what they were saying and Papo goes home to do his assignment:

To Live and Die in Spanish Harlem

His name was Papo.
We didn't know his real name.

He was born with a plastic spoon
melting in his mouth.

His face was carved from marble.

He had silver daggers for eyes.

His heart was shaped like a green toy soldier,
ready to attack.

He had hawk wings attached to his brains.

He crawled to the corner and started running
after his death.

He played follow the leader by himself.

He lived and died in Spanish Harlem.

III.

During an interview to promote his first book, Papo was asked to describe his style. He thought conga, Santeria ritual, black-on-black crime, Cheo Feliciano singing "El Raton," the violent *El Vocero* headlines, and finally decides to use his block. He says, "It's a lot like the mother who sticks her head out the window to call her children in for the night. The way she sings, 'Mira Chino, Marisol y Yoli! Pa'rreeeba! Ahora! Upstairs! Right now!' And the children yell, 'But Maa-ah... Everybody is going to the night-pool and— ,' and she fills in the blanks with: 'and night-pool nothing. Let's go. Get your butts upstairs'. After much pouting and stomping, crying and complaining, Chino and his sisters disappear through the lobby doors. I know this mother. She's like Mami Cuca. She's the mother who consistently has an answer for the Channel 5 newscaster when he asks, 'It's 10:00pm. Do you know where your children are?' And Mami Cuca says, 'My son is in his room sleeping right now, Bill.'"

IV.

Before Papo begins teaching his workshop at the Phoenix House drug program, he gives the participants a brief self-disclosure. "The Hawk was out the night my life changed. He was rocking icicle-shaped sideburns and had a wicked wind chill on his back. I walked out my building and Dona Rosa was pushing her shopping cart up the handicap ramp. She blessed me and told me to be careful on Lexington Avenue because 'it was hot out there.' I heard that a grapevine warning went out to all street-level scramblers engaged in hand-to-hand combat. Chuck Norris and his partner Chewbaca were in the blue Taurus that night. My eyes were glazed with that first bag note. A silent waterfall was chillin' under my lids. Everything made warm sense. I got high to sell and sold to get high. I saw a badge tinkle in a factory window like a July 4th sparkler. I heard one of my customers say, 'Oye, Papo, I think the boys are about to jump.' Before I realized that I made a direct sale, four car doors slammed one right after the other like a *clave* short of a beat. Black Glocks pointed deadly aim, promising fatal shots if I moved and salvation if I stood frozen. It was the sound of the uptown blue man group delivering my one-way ticket to Central Booking. The package included unlimited time shares and revolving door insurance policies. This was my bullpen therapy appointment. Frustration steam started to rise from the top of my head while the City insulated my stomach with inch-thick slices of baloney and American cheese. I've slept through seven-hour trips across the Atlantic Ocean and woken up as the plane descended on the Orly runway in Paris, France. I've been on long, hot yellow school bus rides with a bunch of preschoolers yelling all the way to Jones Beach. And I've been on a comfortable, United Kingdom, cruise-controlled ride in an elegant Mercedes Benz taxi, *Kind of Blue* providing the soundtrack for the awesome countryside vista. But the longest ride I've ever been on was as the sole passenger in the back of a New York Police Department caged bus, hands cuffed in front of me, feeling every second it took to cross the long, white sand bridge that separates Rikers Island from the rest of the world. I remembered being in my lobby and a bunch of us were collecting change for a sponge ball and Duke was talking about going to jail like a college bound senior anticipating the first day of class at the school of his choice. *When I go to jail I'm gonna be like...* Flavors and clicks were the most valuable commodities on the Island. (Newport cigarettes and jack time on the phone.) I called Mami Cuca with my first click and as soon as she heard my voice she cried and said, 'Papo, I would go to the end of the world for you.' I couldn't talk because I swallowed too many heartbeats. I sold a six minute click for a sheet of paper, a pencil and a stamped envelope. I wrote my girlfriend. I told her that I missed the way orange-blossom lotion moistens in her bellybutton and the way she could compress love into seventeen syllables. I made a promise to stop looking at black and white photographs of jazz heroes because they made a fall look sweet and cool. I also told her that I would stop feeding the wind that takes all the lives in the urban studies and that from now on I would use true colors to write about what I know."

Coda: Reflections on the Metro-North, Spring 1997

Monday morning and I'm on the 11:12 from Poughkeepsie to Grand Central.

I'm on my way to let Judge Alderberg know that I went to go tell it on a mountain.

The sun is following this updated reflection.

Doors close on the steam whispers to my gospel hum of I'm starting all over again.

Like the seagulls skipping on the Hudson I know where the wind is taking me these days.

Mad nights I spent on this train going backward.

My jukebox love song girl used to sleep on my shoulder as I watched ducks dance in the street and wished that I could start over.

Sing Sing walls play a song in electrocuted time handcuffed to locked up verses.

Had I stood on the express this would have been my stop.

Corporate card has an office sitting on his lap.

My stomach does a somersault as we creep up on a Bronx that used to be burnt down. It's building blocks for the future now.

I grab my mental mops from my soul bucket.

We need to clean this land of smoke shops, death in hip-hops and black justice in the hands of white cops.

No more poems about dead end screams and ain't nobody hear shit.

Doors close too slow on 125th Street.

Mickey Mouse is about to open a spot on Seventh Avenue.

Steam starts to do a slow ohhh shit you see that blue, dusty Taurus parked behind the school yard?

TNT is eight deep, don't sleep — to be aware is to survive.

Signals are in sync for a direct sale bust on 123rd Street.

The train rumbles by the bodega where a crew of cold turkeys attacked my panic buttons and made me pawn my passport.

From corner to corner moves my old fortuneteller.

On 122nd Street Mami Cuca is sitting on her beach chair composing state-of-the-block speeches with Miss Mary.

Next stop: Times are Square for real.

Curbs have PG ratings.

Make sure you take your personal belongings and leave the past where it belongs.

Remember to tell Alderberg that today my ghost got arrested in front of a bodega.

Don't forget what Colin said during Inspirational Hour: Religion is for people who are afraid to go to hell; spirituality is for people who been there.

Bopping back into the seed of this strange fruit I take out a prayer, puff on some peace and put some in the stash for later.

RESIDUE

Kicking

Skipping rocks on a
Lisbon Falls lake,
my cousin told me to
stop wishing for
a magic potion that
will make me stop.
But peep this for a taste:
On the one hand
picture yourself burping
yellow tops for breakfast.
You're down with the
seven dwarves whereby
you owe you owe you
owe you owe you owe.
The boys been showing
everyone around the block
your mug shot and you
couldn't buy the tombstone
your mother picked out because
her insurance money
was in your pocket and the
next thing you know it
turned into a meteor.
On the other hand,
picture yourself waiting for
your son to come out of school
so you could go skip rocks.
When you stop at the
house you find out that
you're going to have another
child and this time your wife
thinks it's a boy because the cow

lick at the top of your son's
head is going clockwise.
Your son asks you why you
like skipping rocks so
much and you say
because one day you made
a flat stone skip almost
ten times while your
cousin drew a picture of
your life with his hands.

Look What I Found

So I was walking
to a reading
when I saw these
two brothers
talking in front
of a church.

Brother One was
talking about his
platonic relationship
with Jesus,
Sunday miracles,
and baptized dreams.
He said, I pray.
I pray every day
and I pray every
night.

Brother Two egged
him on with a
speak and a say
that.

Then Brother
One said, You
hear me? I
pray every
night.

When he saw
me approaching,
he lowered his voice
to a hymn,
waited until I
passed by and
said, Even
when I'm high.

Trago

Some of us stopped going to the parlors since Petey. Chuna stays outside because he gets nightmares when he steps into the same room with a casket. Jimmy cracks the first pint of dark and says B got mad dust in his system now because B was a dust head and a lot of those stamps out right now brush embalming fluid on their mint leaves.

Junior pulled out the Polaroid we took during that block party when Clyde put his head down to think and the next thing you know he was dead on his back staring at the sky. It was me, Junior, B, Ray, Payito, Sinbad, Bam Bam, and B was looking at the camera like a coyote who wants you to think he's smiling. He had his Dirty Harry aimed at the lens. It was the last group shot of a death squad that had stopped talking about the latest dances.

When all the plastic cups are filled, Loco Tommy gives a quick shout to God and he calls him *Papa Dio.* "Look out for B. We sending him correct. He got the gold rope wrapped around his hands and he ain't got on boots so he should be okay to get in." Everybody takes a *trago* at the same time and then someone started talking about monsters. Loco Tommy squashed it. If anyone asks, he says, it was cancer. Everything is cancer.

Un Amor de la Calle

Last Friday night I was walking down Lexington and Truth called me from across the street and said he had something to tell me. Before I got to the corner he said, "Whaddup, nigga. Ain't seen you in awhile. Act like you don't know nobody." I told him I was working on some fiction. He said, 'That don't mean you can't call a brother, send him a note or something." Lie came out of the bodega, walking sideways. He put a box of strawberry Phillie blunts in his pocket, gave me a weak-ass power grip and said the jump-off was ready. Deceit was chilling by the corner phone telling Duplicity that if his wife comes around looking for him tell her that he got arrested, and that he'll be in Central Booking for the weekend. Fidelity was doing push-ups on the WALK, DON'T WALK traffic light. Sincerity stuck her head out of a window and told him to come down from there, dinner was ready. Dishonesty pulled up in a black beamer with South Carolina plates. He was recruiting for a drive-by on some old beef. Reason called me from across the street and told me not to forget the church bus ride to Atlantic City on Sunday. Connivance was standing behind a dumpster, putting bricks in a VCR box. Honesty waved to me from the back of a M101 that was going downtown, said I should use her number. Spit was falling from the corner of Scheme's mouth when he told me about his plan to make lots and lots of ducats and that's when Collusion came over and said, If, of course, you still doing that kinda thing.